Legendary Tales
for Children

GOPU
BOOKS

An Imprint of V&S PUBLISHERS

Published by:

BOOKS

An Imprint of

F-2/16, Ansari Road, Daryaganj, New Delhi-110002
☎ 011-23240026, 011-23240027 • *Fax:* 011-23240028
Email: info@vspublishers.com • *Website:* www.vspublishers.com

Regional Office : Hyderabad
5-1-707/1, Brij Bhawan (Beside Central Bank of India Lane)
Bank Street, Koti, Hyderabad - 500 095
☎ 040-24737290
E-mail: vspublishershyd@gmail.com

Follow us on:

For any assistance sms **VSPUB** to **56161**

All books available at **www.vspublishers.com**

© **Copyright:** *V&S* PUBLISHERS
ISBN 978-93-505708-3-8
Edition 2014

Printed at : Param Offseters, Okhla, New Delhi-110020

publisher's notes

V&S Publishers has been in the forefront in publishing story books for children - under the imprint Gopu Books. Most books are educational, moral and value-based in nature. Nearly every book published under this imprint has been lapped up by parents and guardians on behalf of their children, both in English and Hindi versions. Since the dawn of time, parents have used stories with morals to teach children about the values of the family, about life, difference between right and wrong, good and bad. A story with a moral can help, more so contemporary ones with which children can relate conveniently. Unlike most prevalent books in the market that exist only for their entertainment value, this book **Legendary Tales for Children** offers to build strength of character and respect for others.

This book is a compilation of 50 one-page stories for children. Language used is elementary and simple. Each story comes with caricature based illustration in black & white – a presentation no other publisher has attempted before. Being different from the ordinary run of the mills type, the caricatures retain interest of young readers. The moral at the end of the story summaries precisely what the child is supposed to learn!

By reading stories, children will gather how characters deal with situations and work through issues, they gain experience without having to go through those conditions themselves. Their horizon is expanded that fits the ethos and mores of a traditional society like ours.

We would be glad to receive feedback from parents so that future publications retain the flavour of enlightened views that expand horizon of our young readers.

----

contents

silence of a beggar

One fine day King Akbar called his court members to discuss a very important question, 'if one has an encounter with a worthless and ill-mannered person, then what would be the right way of dealing with him?' Someone in his court replied- one must beat a person like this in order to make him go away. And some other person in court said- one must imprison such an insolent individual. This discourse was going on suddenly, Beerbal entered the court. Therefore King asked same question to him. To that Beerbal replied- 'Your Majesty! This is indeed a very serious question. It requires a lot of reflection and deep evaluation, only then I can provide you with an answer tomorrow.' And the King agreed to his term.

The very next day when Beerbal entered the court there was a man accompanying him. The man was bare-feet and was wearing an ordinary dress which wrapped his body. Beerbal addressed the King and said-'Your Majesty! This person here is a very wise beggar. He is learned enough to answer your question. The King put his question across to this wise beggar. But the beggar did not answer King's question. Then it occurred to king, maybe he did not get his question right. Therefore he repeated his question. Even then the beggar did not answer him. Now the King thought, maybe he has got some difficulty in hearing properly, so the King asked again in a very loud voice. Then Beeerbal had to intervene and he said, 'Your Majesty! His answer remains in his silence itself. One must not entertain such a person. If one encounters such a fellow, then it is important to practice silence.' The great King Akbar became very pleased after getting Beerbal's clever reply. And the King praised Beerbal to a great deal in his court.

Moral

Silence is the answer to a baseless question.

an eternal king

King Pratap Rai had only one concern for his subjects that is nobody should remain unhappy in his kingdom. The king would leave no edge in the up keep and security of his subjects. The subjects in his kingdom were very happy with their king and they would leave no chance to prove it to their beloved king. One day a group of sages came to this city. To see king's dedication towards everyone, the sages decided to organize a twenty one days prayer ritual to honour the city and the king, which will make the king eternal. All the subjects of this kingdom were asked to give offerings for this ritual. On the twenty first day the king was required to come himself in order to give final offering. After getting the consent from king all necessary arrangements were made, the alter was set where the offerings were to be placed and with a lot of determination the ritual started.

Such a grand ritual can only happen once in a while. That is why people participated in it with a lot of enthusiasm and generously contributed for such a noble cause happily. Every subject of this happy kingdom gave offerings with great zeal and dedication. And finally the last day arrived. Everyone was waiting for King Pratap Rai to arrive, because after giving his final offering he would be made eternal, as the one who would never be dead. Finally the king reached but it was long after the auspicious time had ended. The king asked for pardon in front of his subject and said, 'without any warning our neighbouring country had attacked us. I had to defeat our enemy hence I went to the battle field to give them a good fight. In the greed of becoming eternal I could not have put my country men and their lives in danger.' His praise was sung everywhere that even it was echoing in the sky. Such a king will always remain and remembered as the most efficient ruler in the eyes of his subjects eternally.

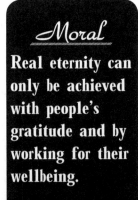

Moral

Real eternity can only be achieved with people's gratitude and by working for their wellbeing.

9

authority and duty

King Yashovardan decided used to change his garb and used to go out in disguise to know how his subjects were living in his state. One day the king got into his disguise and went out on an inspection. He saw a band of people were beating up a person and they were dragging him to some place. King stopped someone and asked why was this person being beaten up? That person told him, the man who was being beaten up was a poor man; he lifted food from some shop and ate it without paying for it, and the person who is beating him up is the shopkeeper himself. Then king asked his next question where he was taken to? He was told the man was taken to the city police station where police in charge will be resting comfortably for sure. After listening to all this immediately king dropped of his garb and showed his appearance as a king. As soon as the shop keeper recognised it was king he stopped beating that man and the poor man fell on king's feet. King held him and lifted him from the ground and said, 'Friend, did you steal because of your poverty, it means you were not taken care off and police chief rather than inspecting is sitting comfortably in the police station, also it means I was unable to protect you and this shop keeper had to responsibility of justice in his hands...' for all my wrong approach I ask for forgiveness from you.

This is how great kings used to discover how his subjects are living. Sending some messengers to find out the truth may bring incorrect reports. This practice of kings going incognito to know how people live has been in existence in India for many years.

Moral

With authority it is the responsibility of the ruler to project people's interests, this is how he can perform his duty well.

cleverness of the king

*H*aving learnt about king Vikramjeets's cleverness, the head of all the Gods, God Indra decided to take a test of this king. Lord Indra sent three heads of human beings and said if he could tell the worth of these heads, he will bestow rain of gold over his kingdom. Even his court members could not answer this question to the king. Finally the king asked the same question to the priest.

At night the priest told everything to his wife. She became worried. During this time Shiva and Parvati were roaming the Earth. When Parvati saw priest's wife in trouble she requested Lord Shiva to help her. Shiva and Parvati in the shape of a male and female jackal reached toward her. The wife heard jackal talking. She decided to hide under a tree. The male jackal spoke 'do you know Lord Indra has sent three heads to test the worth of the king Vikramjeet. If he could tell their real worth there will be a golden shower on this kingdom or else everything will get destroyed. I know the actual worth of all three heads. I will tell you this secret. Put a golden needle through all three heads, if the needle does not get through ears, nose or mouth that head is very precious. The head through which golden needle comes out of the mouth its worth ten thousand only. And the head through which needle passes from every part its worth is two only.

Listening this she went home and told everything to her husband. Next day in the court the priest called for all three heads. He demostrated to the king the worth of each head as per the discussion the jackals were having. King wrote the worth of every head and sent it to Lord Indra. God Indra got very happy with his answers and there was a golden shower throughout this kingdom and the priest got his desired rewards.

Moral

A person who uses and knows the worth of his senses through his eyes, nose and mouth is the wisest one.

the forest of sandal wood

A king went far ahead one day while hunting in the jungle. On his way back he lost his way. It was dark already. At a distance he saw a small hut. He called for someone in the hut. There came a man from inside. He was poor. King requested him to let him stay for one night. As much as he could do he arranged for the comfort for the king. Before leaving the king asked him his source of income.

The man replied, 'Your Majesty, I cut wood from the jungle and burn them to make charcoal, and this is how I get my daily bread.' The king was very happy with this person's hospitality. He gave him a part of his sandalwood forest.

Time passed away and one day the king decided to visit his sandalwood forest. He went to see it. The king got a shock of his life. The whole forest had depleted and that person was also living his days in poverty. King asked him 'what did you do with my sandalwood forest?'

He replied, 'Your Majesty earlier I would go too far of places to get wood and made charcoal out of it. But this sandalwood forest was nearby so I started chopping its wood to make charcoal. I have cut down all the trees now only one tree is left.

The King become sad and said 'you are very foolish, you did not understand importance of a sandalwood forest. This forest and its wood could have made you rich. Now from the tree which is left cut a branch from it and go sell it in the market.' That person did what he was told. In return of that small piece of wood he has got a lot of money. To have seen this now he lamented on his foolishness and asked king to forgive him.

King tried to explain that there is no use feeling sad about it. Now you have learnt the value of a sandalwood forest. Now keep on selling small chunks of wood and earn good money. And plant more trees of sandalwood from now on till the forest grows back again.'

Moral

Foolish people can never understand worth of anything valuable. They cannot differentiate between a piece of glass or diamond.

teaching of a sage

There was a king. All his court members had only one task which was to please their king forever. Whatever the king would do his court members would do the same. One day there were heavy clouds in the sky. The king said 'the night has fallen'. Entire court shouted, 'Yes Sir, the night has fallen.'

One day out of sheer luck a holy sage arrived in the court. He had a very long beard and a big moustache. The king had a very strong dislike towards moustache and beard. He ordered his men to throw away the sage from his court. His men immediately followed his orders. Many days passed since this incidence. And one day the king went into the forest on a hunting expedition. There was a small shack in this forest in which lived the holy sage. King kept on waiting for an animal to appear but there came none. He arrived at the spot where the shack of the sage was. He could not remember this holy sage. The sage was very hospitable to the king. He offered fruits to the king. And the king felt very nice. He spoke, 'I am the king oh holy sage! If you have any wish do tell me. I will make sure you get your wish.

The sage spoke, 'Your Majesty! Once I was a king like you. One day I realised there is nothing in this world which belongs to us. Neither we do not come with anything nor we leave anything behind. Therefore, I left everything and arrived here. Which satisfies me so much'.

The king realised immediately that it was the same sage whom he had disrespected and threw out of his court. He realised the court members cunning nature. I cannot differentiate between right or wrong. The king was engrossed in his thoughts. But the sage was saying, 'Your Majesty, it is very difficult to attain a human life. A real human is the one whose knowledge plexus are working all the time and he lives in this world but somehow he is always above it in seeing and understanding things.' When king returned to his palace he felt the human being within his body has finally woken up and the king was self-absorbed is no more.

Moral

Don't fall for flattery; use your own instinct to decide what is good.

goodness in charity

*O*nce upon a time there was a king. He was a very intelligent as well as a very superior being. He was never defeated by anyone in his life. He had a very beautiful wife. One day the king asked one of his royal teachers, 'Sir, whatever I have earned in this life with honesty and good deeds, I want to earn more goodness so that in my next life I will attain more wealth, opulence and popularity because of my good deeds.'

His royal teacher replied, 'Your Highness! Years ago there was a pious lady she had devoted all her time in praying and worshiping God sincerely. You were that lady's helper in your past life. She spent everything in doing charity. She had a golden tree made on which there were golden flowers and it bore statues of gods and goddesses on it. You helped that lady in building up the golden tree selflessly. And when the lady offered you money for your services you refused to accept it. You said to her it was done in the path of righteousness. And your wife along with you helped her to polish golden leaves and flowers of this tree. In this life as well she is your wife too. Your Majesty! You have attained all this opulence and goodness because of your hard work for a greater cause.'

Further the royal teacher spoke, 'in those days you were an ordinary person. But now you are a king therefore you must do charity and give away at least a heap of grain which should be as big as a mountain. When you could attain so much in this life due to your hard work for a nobler cause as an ordinary person then you can imagine as a king if you give charity of food grains as the size of a mountain how much you will be rewarded in your next life with.' The king understood what this royal teacher implied and he followed what he was asked for.

He started giving money and other useful things to the needy people without thinking about returns. He grew to become ever more wealthy. Because of his helpful nature he was liked by everyone in his state.

8

the one who sees is more blind

*O*ne day Akbar asked Beerbal, 'Tell me who are the people more in numbers in this word, those who can see everything or those who are blind?' Beerbal replied 'the blind people are more in number.' Akbar asked 'how is that possible? Can you prove that you are right?' To the king Beerbal replied 'right now I cannot prove myself right but give me two days' time'. The very next day Beerbal went to the market and sat there with an un-knitted cot and started knitting it then and there. He made two men sit with him with a pen and paper. To see Beerbal sitting in the crowded market many people gathered there. Everyone present there was asking only one question from Beerbal- 'Beerbal what exactly are you doing?'Both the men sitting on each side of Beerbal were noting down names of people who were asking this question.

When King learnt that Beerbal was busy knitting a cot right in the middle of a market place he also went there to see him. He immediately asked Beerbal, 'what are you doing here?' Without answering to him Beerbal asked one man sitting next to him to note down King Akbar's name in the list after listening to this king snatched away the paper from the man's hand. On that piece of paper was written- A List of Blind Men. King asked 'what is this all about and why have you written my name in it?' Beerbal replied, 'Your Highness! You have seen that I am knitting a cot here, even then you have asked what am I doing here? You very well can see from your eyes but you asked what I was doing? Therefore you must agree with what I have said the other day, that there are more blind people in number than those who can really see? On Beerbal's cleverness King smiled quietly.

This true story of Akbar-Beerbal has an underlying meaning. We say so many things out of sheer habit, without thinking, without analysing. Its is always wise to see, think and then say what you need to say.

Moral

There are such blinded people in this world who questions despite seeing thing.

how beerbal caught a thief

*K*ing Akbar was very fond of jewels. In the king's palace there were at least eight such servants who would keep his clothes and jewellery in proper form. No one was allowed to enter Akbar's royal chamber. One day Akbar decided to wear his favourite ring. But it was nowhere to be found. Akbar got very angry after learning that it was lost. He ordered his staff to find his favourite ring immediately. After a lot of effort that ring was nowhere to be found. In the end Akbar decided to call Beerbal and said to him, 'that ring was very dear to me. I want that ring back to me at any cost.' Beerbal said, 'Your Majesty! Do not worry because soon you will be able to wear your favourite ring in your finger again.'

Beerbal called all eight servants, who would go to Akbar's royal chamber. Beerbal gave each one of them similar sized and shaped piece of wood and asked them to bring it tomorrow with them, he told them which ever servant has stolen this ring of the king his piece of wood will grow on its own an inch more in the night. Next day all eight servants stood in a row holding their piece of wood in their respective hands. Amongst those eight servants one was taken by Birbal to the king Akbar. That servant fell in Akbar's feet and confessed his crime because he was the one who stole this ring. But king was very amazed. He asked Beebal how he managed to find the thief. Beerbal told him everything and in the end said 'Your Majesty! Due to the fear of being caught he has cut his piece of wood by an inch this is how he was caught.' King applauded Birbal in his court and gave due punishment to this thief.

Nearly every thief leaves behind one clue or another of his act. A wise and intelligent person can use his brain to discover the person who has committed the time. Modern police tries to catch the thieves in the similar manner.

Moral
While committing a crime every culprit leaves some source of information behind and because of it he gets caught.

tenaliraman's horse

*K*ing Krishnadev Rai had very nice collection of horses which were of higher breed. Whenever he would sell them off he could make good money out of them. To see this transaction happen Tenaliraman would grow sadder. He also had one horse but it was frail and weak. That is why nobody wanted to buy it.

One day Tenaliraman and King Krishnadev went for horse riding on their respective horses. During their excursion king saw Tenaliraman's weak horse and said 'what kind of frail horse you have? Why don't you sell it in some nitty-gritty price?' after listening to this Tenaliraman said 'why should I sell my horse in nitty-gritty price when I am already getting good prices for it. You know it is very efficient horse. All the work it can do for you, not even your horse can perform. If you wish you can try it.' After listening to him Krishnarai got really angry and said 'there is no such work which my horse cannot do. For this reason we will have a bet for hundred gold pieces at least. The one who will lose has to pay hundred gold pieces to the winner.' Tenaliraman agreed to his conditions.

After a certain distance they saw a river. Tenaliraman saw the flow of the river and its current was quite a fast. He did not pay any attention here or there but forced his horse in the river. Now he asked Krishnadev Rai, 'Your Highness can your horse do this?' The king pushed his horse into the river. Unfortunately the horse, got drowned in the fast current of river. And he paid Tenaliraman hundred gold pieces in return. After accepting the gold pieces Tenaliraman grew very happy on his ability so to say on his cleverness. He returned home happily.

Moral

Sometimes even a less valuable thing can get good profit.

25

a dream of akbar

*O*ne night Akbar had a dream where he saw all his teeth have fallen except one. To understand the meaning of this dream he called all his royal astrologers to interpret this dream of his. He told them about this particular dream of his and asked them, 'why do you think I have had this dream and what does it mean or what could be the reason behind it?' To his query astrologers replied 'it means before your death your relatives will be dead.' After listening to it Akbar grew very worried. Without rewarding them he asked his astrologers to go away and they all returned just the way they came.

After some time Birbal entered his court. He saw Akbar sitting in deep thought and looked worried. He asked, 'Your Majesty! What is the matter with you? Why are you looking so worried?' Akbar told him about his dream and also told him about what interpretation his astrologers had given him. After listening to him Birbal spoke very cleverly 'I can interpret your dream for you rightly. And it means you will live longer than any of your relative.' When he heard this clever interpretation Akbar smiled at Birbal's smartness and rewarded him in front of his court.

It is said that even bad news can be presented in a way that doesn't offend the emotion of the lister. Whichever way you interpret it, the outcome would be the same. Nevertheless, presenting a sad news or happening in a subtle and soft way is what we should practic in daily life. Just the way Birbal did.

Moral
To announce a bad news with some consideration and positivity can make worst thing sound better. To hear such a thing does not make a person feel bad at all.

12

hearty maize

Rampur's King was on an inspection one day. After a daylong work when he was returning he saw there stood a field which had a beautiful crop of maize. Such nice and thick cobs of maize King never saw in his entire life. He asked his attendant 'What is this?' The attendant said 'Sir it is maize.' King said again 'But I have seen such brilliant corn for first time in my life.' On king's demand attendant plucked some corns and roasted them to be served to the king. Every kernel of this maize was delicious. Next day king called for the owner of this maize field. And the king spoke, 'I summoned you here to pay for that maize which I have got plucked yesterday from your fields. But also tell me how maize is so nice and delicious in your field? Whereas in other's fields corns are really scanty and they have fewer kernels on them.'

The farmer's name was 'Manbhar'. He said 'Your Majesty! All I know that my family works really hard on this field. Every year I witness a great harvest and I never hoard even a bit of tax each year.' Then the king said, 'every farmer works hard and they also pay their taxes on time but still their crop is not as good as yours. Maybe you do not want to disclose the right reason to me.' Manbhar said, 'then Your Majesty! Another reason could be when my family works on this field they work very happily and they work with a lot of satisfaction. While sowing seeds my wife always give her gratitude to the mother earth and at the time of irrigation my son obliges God of sky for sending bounties of rain by folding his hands. And when our harvest is about to be ready we all pray that our small field can satisfy hunger of several people by a hearty morsel.'

King said 'hearty' 'that is the reason why maize is so delicious in your fields.' And king paid for his share of hearty maize and let go of the farmer from his court.

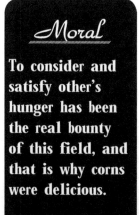

Moral

To consider and satisfy other's hunger has been the real bounty of this field, and that is why corns were delicious.

king indrasen's justice

King Indrasen had a very peculiar habit of eating fresh fish every day. One day a storm struck the sea. That day not even a single fisherman went into the sea to catch any fish. That is why king could not get fresh supply of fish to eat. King announced that whosoever will go in the sea to catch fresh fish today will get a good reward. When a poor fisherman heard this announcement he decided to go by putting his life in jeopardy. After catching few fish he reached the royal palace. King's guard ushered him inside the palace.

The minister told him one thing, 'I can take you in front of the king but on one condition. Whatever reward king will give you, you have to share half of it with me.' The fisherman did not like the minister's proposal but still he agreed on his terms. A guard escorted fisherman in the king's chamber. King was extremely happy to see the fish. He asked the fisherman 'tell me what reward you desire?' fisherman said 'You're majesty! Please lash at least fifty hunters on my back. Only this would be my reward.' Hearing the fisherman speak like this all court members were shocked. Then king asked his helper to strike the fisherman with fifty strokes of hunter but with a light hand. As soon the count reached twenty five the fisherman asked him to stop, and said 'now remaining lashes should go the back of my partner.' King asked fisherman 'who is your partner?,' 'Your minister is my partner sir.' Said the fisherman. After hearingabout everything king became very angry. And he asked his helper to strike the minister with twenty five lashes that too heavily in the court. The minister received the reward of his greed. After which king gave fisherman his desired reward happily.

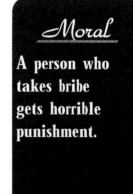

Moral

A person who takes bribe gets horrible punishment.

cost of turban

King Vishvadev was the biggest tyrant of his time. To get people killed was the matter of great pleasure for him. One day in front of him a lot of prisoners were captured and brought in front of him. In which there was a very remarkable poet of Turkistan called 'Ahmedy'. King addressed Ahmedy and said, 'I have heard that poets are very ingenious people. They know the exact value of a person.' Ahmedy nodded his head in a gesture of 'yes'. King pointed towards two slaves and asked him, 'can you tell me their exact values?' Ahmedy was a very fearless and a self-resilient poet of his time. He looked towards the slaves and said, 'their values are not more than five hundred gold coins.'

That was very apt. Then king asked 'now tell me, what would be the exact cost of mine?' Ahmedy replied, 'Twenty five gold coins.' Hearing this a king got enraged. He said in his anger, 'these slaves who are lesser than me are worth five hundred gold coins and my value is only fifty gold coins? It seems you do not love your life. Do you know that is the cost of my turban alone?' Ahmedy said hurriedly 'I have only told you the cost of your turban only. Without it you have no existence or position.'

King understood what Ahmedy implied. He did not kill Ahmedy and allowed him to go by calling him a mad freak. But deep down in his heart he knew other that his turban he has no value.

This king had become the king after his father's death. He didn't have to win wars or defeat enemies to attain the throne. It came to him by birth.

Was he to work to achive the throne he would have known the price or value of a person.

It is wisely said that it is not the king as a person, but the throne that differentials between him and other mortals.

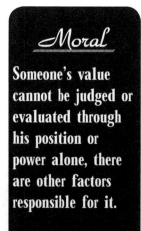

Moral

Someone's value cannot be judged or evaluated through his position or power alone, there are other factors responsible for it.

cleverness of tenaliraman

The sultan of Beejapur, Adilshah had a fear, that someday Krishnadev was trying to snatch away his kingdom from him. Therefore he thought there was only one thing possible, to save his kingdom. He needs to get king Krishnadev killed. To carry such a gruesome task, Adilshah chose the most trusted person of Krishnadev who was Tenaliraman. But it was difficult to persuade Tenaliraman for such an act that is why the Sultan approached his childhood friend Kankuraju and offered him a heavy sum of reward as his promise. He made him peruse Tenaliraman to assassinate the king.

So one day Kankuraju arrived at Tenaliraman's house. Tenaliraman welcomed his friend and gave him space to live in his house. The next day when Tenaliraman was not at home, then Kankuraju sent a message addressing the king on behalf of Tenaliraman. 'Your Highness! You must come at my house as soon as possible. I would like to show you something so marvellous which you might have not seen ever in your life time.' After receiving such a message king arrived at Tenaliraman's house. As soon as he entered his house Kankuraju attacked the king from behind. But king was very alert and as soon as he was attacked he hit back the opponent immediately.

King perceived that Tenaliraman was a part of some conspiracy that is why he announced a punishment for him and decided him to get him killed. Hearing such a punishment Tenaliraman appealed for mercy in front of king but the king did not budge. When Tenaliraman told him the entire truth then king said, 'I cannot forgive you because you have kept a conspirator in your house hence the crime is unpardonable but I can do one thing you may chose the way you would like to die.'

Tenaliraman was a very clever person he said, 'I want such a death which comes with old age.' To have heard such a thing entire court was amazed. And the king smiled at Tenaliraman's cleverness and said. 'Well this time you saved yourself Tenaliraman.'

Moral

A clever person can come out of any trouble.

35

the biggest jewel

King Bheemsingh was extremely proud of his wealth. One day an old friend of his Shamsher came to visit him. To see his friend after a long time the king was very happy. After welcoming his friend king started to show off his palace and opulence to his friend. While showing his place he took Shamsher to his room. There to see all jewels Shamsher's eyes were dazzling with their glare. King started telling him costs. He also told him for the security of these precious jewels he has appointed several soldiers as guards. They guard this place twenty four hours. Shamsher was listening to king's talk but he was least interested in it.

After listening to the king for a long time Shamsher asked him, 'tell me one thing friend! You have so much of wealth but does it benefit others?' king replied, 'with so many precious jewels why should others be benefiting? They all are for me alone.' Shasher took the king to a small hut. Where an old woman used to live she used to grind flour for living.

Shamsher showed king the flour mill and said 'all the jewels in your room are actually stones and this grinding mill is also made up of stone. With all those stones no one can benefit other than you, but this flour mill gives flour to the entire village. To protect those jewels you have to appoint several soldiers but this stone mill does not need any one to guard it. That is why for me this flour mill is more precious than your entire collection of jewels.' After listening to Shamsher king came to know that this flour mill was the biggest asset which this poor old woman had.

It is said that all the precious gold, silver and other gems can't give you even one morsel of food to fill the stomach. These are good only for show and opulence. They don't do any good go the society. Therefore, anything that ordinary people can benefit from can be called useful rest others are useless.

Moral

The biggest object is the one which can benefit the others. Like the old woman's mill.

mulla nasruddin's feast

*O*ne day Mulla Nasruddin was called for a feast as a special guest. He read his invitation and thought that this place is so far away but why thinking so much when the invitation is for a feast. So he decided to go for the party. Whatever clothes Mulla used to wear he reached for this invitation is the same costume. He did not consider changing clothes at all. When he reached to the venue in his bad and sweaty clothes then the door keeper did not let him pass. Mulla told this door keeper that I bear an invitation for this feast and I am today's special guest. All door men started to laugh at him and disrespected him by throwing him away.

A little further from there Mulla's friend Rehman used to live. He went to Rehman's place. His friend got very happy to see him because he happened to arrive by chance. After knowing each other's well being Mulla asked his friend, 'Brother! Do you remember that red cloak of yours, which you wanted to give as a present to me?' Rehman said 'sure I remember it.' Mulla asked hesitatingly, 'Do you have that cloak still with you?' Rehman said, 'yes it still with me. If you want you can take it from me'. He said 'yes I want it but will you ask me to return it to you?' Rehman replied, 'Oh no, what I gave you as a present I could never ask you back.' Mulla thanked Rehman and wore his new cloak and arrived for the feast.

In that red cloak he appeared not any less than a wealthy man. All the door men saluted him and escorted him inside the banquet hall. All the people were waiting there for Mulla to arrive. And Mulla's veneration started with great hospitality. First they offered him a bowl of soup. Mulla rose up with his bowl and poured entire bowl on his cloak. To see this everyone was stunned. And their jaws dropped then and there. One person asked him 'Mulla why did you do that? The soup was for you not for your cloak to have.' The door men were standing there Mulla looked at them and said to his cloak 'I hope you enjoyed your soup very well. It was especially for you. They have called you for this feast, not me.' To have heard his remark all door keeper's head fell in shame and they asked for forgiveness to Mulla.

Moral

With good looking clothes never judge a person's greatness, on the contrary one must analyse his good qualities.

a poor man's sack

One day Mulla was going somewhere. He saw a man on the road. He was sitting and cursing his destiny. He was complaining to God why he made him so poor? Mulla reached to him to ask 'Brother why are you crying so much?' the poor man showed him his worn out sack and said 'I do not have this much of belonging which can come inside this worn out sack of mine. All I have in life is this worn out sack.' Mulla felt quite sad after seeing the condition of this man. All of a sudden he snatched that sack from this poor man's hand and started to run away from him.

To see his only belonging being taken away the poor man started to cry even louder. Now he was sadder than before. But what he could have done now. By feeling sad he started to walk ahead on his road. And further Mullah has placed his sack right in the middle of the same road. As soon as the poor man saw his sack he leapt with happiness towards it. To have found his sack again he was so happy that nothing could compare it with other happiness, to have seen him in joy Mulla thought it is a marvellous way of making anyone happy again.

What this story tells us that we are not content with what we have. We always seek more of everything we come to know the worth of a thing only when it is lost or gone. We realise its importance when we get it back.

Afterall wealth like happiness is never attained when sought directly. It comes as a by product of providing a useful service no matter how small.

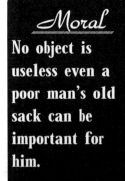

Moral

No object is useless even a poor man's old sack can be important for him.

mulla nasruddin and his coin

*D*ue to times rotation Mulla's luck was also turned. He became poor from being rich. He barely had anything to eat now. One day a thought came in his mind which was, it's better to start begging rather than killing ones hunger. He stood at the city's cross road to beg from people. There was no dearth of people who were jealous of Mulla's good old days. Now to see Mulla begging they found a good opportunity to ridicule him. Every day they would keep one gold coin in front of him and one silver coin. Mulla would say prayers in their favour and would pick the silver coin from there. As soon as he would pick only a silver coin his enemy's would call him a fool.

Right next to Mulla another beggar used to stand with him. He would see Mulla picking up only silver coin every day. One day he asked Mulla, 'Brother! Tell me one thing one gold coin's value is much more than a silver piece's worth, then why would you only pick up silver coin alone and let your enemies laugh at you. Why you do it always?' 'If I will pick up their gold coin from next time on wards they will not give me even one silver coin as well. Every time I let them laugh at me so that I could pick up a silver coin for myself. You know I have collected so much of silver now that I do not have to worry any longer about my every day bread.' After listening to Mulla's remark the beggar understood it was not Mulla who was a fool but actually foolish are those people who laugh at him and to do so every day they throw a silver piece at him.

Mulla knew that greed brings disaster. Nothing is actually gained by becoming greedy. It disturbs peace of mind which ultimately affects health. he was intelligent enough to earn in a small way so that the profit continues for ever.

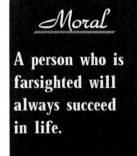

Moral

A person who is farsighted will always succeed in life.

justice of the king

There was a king who used to change his dress at night and would go out to check on his subjects. One night while going around four strangers came to him and asked, 'who are you?' king replied 'I am searching for a livelihood here.' Four strangers felt happy and told him 'we are thieves and we are here to steal something. Would you be interested in our work?' The king desired to know their plan and said yes to them. When they all were about to start one thief said 'we must decide who will perform which task. '

One of them said, 'while stealing the biggest hurdles are dogs. I understand their language and we would be saved from getting caught.' Second one said, 'I can see clearly even in darkness. That is why we will not have to use light for our purpose.' Third one said 'I can even break a strong wall if needed.' And the forth one said 'I can smell even a buried pot of money in the ground.' Now it was king's turn. He said, 'I have a powerful beard. As soon it moves I can pardon anyone's crimes or sins with it.' They plotted their scheme and circled the palace. On their way king extracted their names and where they all lived. As soon as they arrived near the palace one dog barked. First thief replied, 'this dog is saying the king is somewhere near by.' But no one agreed to what he was saying. Second one directed everyone in darkness and took them near treasure. They all showed their stealing talents and looted the whole treasure. Thereafter, they all in different direction and king went inside the palace to alert his soldiers. He gave them their whereabouts. All the thieves were caught and brought before the king. he was sitting in the same garb, in which he has met all these thieves. All four thieves were scared to see the king right in front of them. They started to beg for his mercy. King said to them, 'you all have committed a crime therefore all four of you will be punished.

Then one thief said 'you said you have a powerful beard as soon as it moves anyone's crime may get resolved. So kindly show your talent and pardon all our crimes.' To hear this king smiled and said 'fine I will do so but in future if I see this happening again then I will not pardon any crime of yours.' By now king knew their talents and he appointed them as his soldiers in the palace.

Moral

Every person is endowed with some talent or the other, but its use must always be accommodated for a good work.

the justice of the khalifa

*T*he Khaleefa of Baghdad Harun-al Rasheed was known for his greatness in imparting justice. People would come from far off places to seek his justice.

In the same city there lived a trader named Rehman. So he decided to go on a tour one day. After getting all preparation he was left with a thousand gold coins still. He has put them in a jar and stuffed it with olives on the top. He gave it to his friend Ali to keep it safe with him as his friends belonging. After a year when Rehman returned from his tour he asked Ali to return his jar of olives in which he has stuffed all his gold coins. When he looked into his jar there was no gold coin in it. On the contrary when Rehman asked Ali about it he simply refused knowing anything about it started to say nasty things for Rehman.

Rehman took Ali to Khaleefa to seek justice. After listening to everything Khaleefa asked Ali 'did you take out any gold coin out of the jar?' Ali denied any such act. Due to lack of evidence no solution to this problem was attained. One day Khaleefa was strolling around his house. Then he saw few kids were playing nearby dramatizing the entire episode of Rehman seeking justice. One child was pretending to be Ali and other was pretending to be Rehman. And Khaleefa waited there to see the end of their play.

The kid who was pretending to be Khaleefa said, 'I order to analyse how old are those olives which are lying in this jar.' Then the kid who was Rehman said after smelling them, 'Oh they are not more than two months old.' Then the child spoke who was pretending to be Khaleefa 'but you went on a tour for one entire year? Then how is can be possible for these olives to be only two months stale? This means Ali took out all gold coins from Rehman's jar and stuffed fresh olives in them.' This is how Khaleefa understood how he can give justice after seeing those children act. He summoned Rehman and Ali immediately. And asked to get that particular jar of olives analysed, as soon as the result came out they got to know olives were fresh. This is how Rehman got his justice and Ali received his punishment.

Moral

To give justice one must analyse reality thoroughly and carefully

a clever king

*O*ne business man lugged fifty bundles of cloth to be sold in a different country. He grew very tired and decided to rest under a tree. Due to fatigue he fell asleep. When he woke up from his sleep he was surprised to see all his bundles of clothes and stolen missing from there. He became extremely worried and went to see the king of this country and seek justice. King asked all his subjects to gather at one particular point. When he saw this gathering he said, 'I order everyone to bring at least one bundle of cloth tomorrow. A person who will not follow this order will be put behind bars.'

Next day everyone reached king's palace with a bundle of cloth held by each one of them. The business man started to locate his bundles one by one. He recognised his bundle of cloth and the person who was carrying it was held under custody. After investigation he confessed that he stole it from business man all his bundles of cloth. People were returned their bundles and the thief was given his due punishment. The business man was very pleased with the king's justice and he took all his bundles and went ahead for another city.

We must remember that wherever our individual troubles and challenges, it is important to pause every now and then and appreciate all that we have got on every level. We need to literally 'count our blessings', give thanks for them to everyone who has bestowed even one bit of happiness and allow ourselves to enjoy them, and relish the experience of prosperity we have come to acquire.

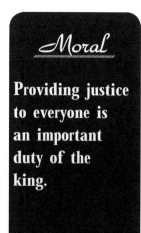

Moral

Providing justice to everyone is an important duty of the king.

ā slap-thapd

One day Mulla Nasriddin was roaming around a market place. All of a sudden a stranger approached him and gave him a one tight slap right on his cheek. Before Mulla could complain the man folded his hands in forgiveness and said, 'you appear to me like one true friend. I thought he was passing from this place. But you turned out to be someone else. Kindly forgive me.'

Mulla did not trust him and decided to take him to the king. Mulla's friend Shamsuddin was waiting around the corner and was seeing all this happening in front of his eyes. Actually he was responsible for sending that man to play a prank on Mulla. But he had no idea that Mulla will take this joke so seriously. He immediately walked towards Mulla and without telling him the truth asked the reason of his anger. Mulla narrated the whole incidence to him. Shamsuddin tried to defend the stranger and said 'Oh dear brother! He did not slap you intentionally. And he was asking for your forgiveness as well. I would recommend that let go of this matter. And if you want you can accept one rupee as part of the compensation from him.'

Mulla was clever in order to know that the stranger and his friend are each other's ally and they together have plotted such a deed. Mulla decided to teach them a lesson and accepted his offer. Shamsuddin asked this stranger, 'you must give a rupee as compensation to Mulla.' The stranger replied 'I do not have one rupee right now but if you allow I can go home to fetch it and can bring it to you.' Shamsuddin replied 'ok get it here we will wait for you.' After he left Shamsuddin went to a nearby shop to sit and started gossiping while being there. But Mulla stood there and he was waiting for the stranger to return.

After a long time's wait the stranger did not return, then Mulla went towards Shamsuddin and said, 'friend do you think that to hit a person one can offer a compensation of one rupee?' Shamsuddin said 'yes it can be because one rupee is not a small amount.' Then Mulla slapped Shamsuddin then and there and said, 'when that stranger would come with the sum of one rupee you can keep it.' He said this much and left the place immediately.

Moral

One must do the same with such a person who causes troubles to the others, this is considered a wise act

a sovereign's righteousness

*I*t is said that that in the region of Magadh a King named Bimbisar ruled whose capital was Kushanagar a strange phenomenon started to take place. Every day one citizen or the other will have his house engulfed in fire. And all the people of this city were very worried with this phenomenon.

One day they all gathered and decided to go to meet the king and said everything to him. To see his subjects' troubles he started to think of various ways to solve this trouble. He addressed the town's men 'if each one of you will try to protect your house then one can overcome this trouble of houses catching fire on their own.' Also he declared that 'if someone's house will get burnt that person will have to move out of the city and live in the jungle on the outerskirts of this town.'

Due to bad luck one day the palace caught fire. And the king left his palace to leave for the forest. All the court members tried hard to prevent him from going to the forest, but the king did not listen to anyone and said, 'what I said for everyone applies to me as well. It was not meant for other citizens only it is equally applicable for me as well. I cannot disobey a rule which I have made for everyone in Kushagnagar, and if I do so then what will I say to my people?'

The king went to the forest to live and his righteousness and justice became more popular amongst his subjects. Over a period of time all the houses got burnt in the kingdom and they all came to live in the forest. It is said that a new kingdom of Magadh was established which grew popular with the name of Rajgraha.

Absolutely speaking do unto others as you would they do unto you. If you makes rules with exceptions, everyone would like to seek exceptions. Make a rule that applies to every person, including yourself. That's called the golden rule.

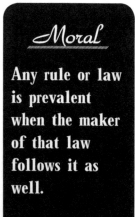

Moral

Any rule or law is prevalent when the maker of that law follows it as well.

25

alexander's pride

*A*lexander defeated the king of Iran. After this triumph he was considered an undefeatable ruler. Now his subjects in his country decided to honour their great king by organising a victory procession for him. From wherever Alexander passed people bowed their heads in the honour of their king.

During the same time Alexander saw a bunch of beggars coming from the other end of the road. He thought that those beggars will stop in order to pay homage to their king. But none of them even looked at him. Alexander considered it as his insult and ordered his soldiers to get those beggars in front of him. When all the beggars were summoned in front of Alexander then he said, 'do you people not know that I am the conqueror of the world? How dare you to insult me like this?'

One of the beggar replied, 'the fake pride and valour you are boasting about, we have renounced it long ago. For us you are just one commoner, not the world conqueror. To hear all this Alexander's face turned red with anger. The beggar spoke again, 'you are still stuck in your deception of pride and valour but for us it is futile and it is of no value. Why are you so full of pride? Can you ever come up to our level? What is your importance before us?'

Therefore Alexander's pride melted then and there like hot wax. That beggar's remark pricked him like a spear but still he accepted his smallness in front of them. In front of those beggars all his achievements of pride were nothing. He asked for forgiveness from all the beggars and released them immediately.

The pride of money, honour and popularity is futile and small in nature, because such qualities can leave a mortal's side any time in the life and they are not permanent.

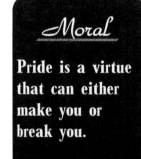

Moral

Pride is a virtue that can either make you or break you.

root of sin

One day emperor Chandrabhaan asked his friend Shursen what is the root cause of every sin? Shursen could not give a satisfactory answer to it. Emperor said 'I will give you one month's time to find a suitable answer to this question. And if you cannot produce a suitable answer in the due time then you have to leave your minister's position for not being able to do so.' Shursen became very worried. He roamed around villages in order to get an answer. One day he lost his way and reached inside a jungle. He saw an ascetic sitting over there. He repeated emperor's question in front of him.

The ascetic replied, 'I am a dacoit who is hiding in this disguise due to the soldiers of the king. But I can give you an answer for your question. For which you have to do me a favour.' Shursen thought no matter what this work is going to be at least he will have a definite answer. He agreed on the dacoit's terms and condition. Then the dacoit said, 'fine then you have to kill the wealthy man of your city and you have to steal all his money and bring it to me after killing him. And if you are successful in your task then I will tell you the answer.'

Shursen got into his ploy and was about to leave. To see him leave the dacoit said, 'think once more what you are going to do. To kill and to steal are both sinful acts.' Shursen said 'I will do anything to save my rank and position, for it I can do anything even a sinful deed.' To hear him say this the dacoit spoke, 'this is right answer to your question. The root of any sin is greed. Due to your position you agreed to kill and steal at the same time which is a sin. To get influenced in such a way by greed a person commits sin always.

Shursen thanked the dacoit and went towards the palace. Next day when he told his answer to the emperor, he grew happy after listening to him. He honoured his minister by bestowing royal ornaments on him.

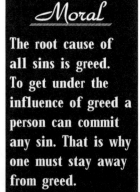

Moral

The root cause of all sins is greed. To get under the influence of greed a person can commit any sin. That is why one must stay away from greed.

mulla nasruddin's donkey

One day Mulla Nasruddin's donkey was stolen. Mulla was utterly confused about who he should trust and who he should suspect. To get his donkey back he put advertisements everywhere even in markets, which read, 'whosoever has stolen my donkey must return it to me, I will give the same donkey to him as a reward.' When people read this advertisement they made huge fun of it. Some people went to the extent of saying Mulla has lost his mind due to the shock of losing his donkey.

People asked him, 'what is the meaning of such announcements or advertisement? Hardly anyone will return your donkey if it got stolen. And think if someone will return it to you. Then you have to give it back to him. Then why are you asking your donkey back? Are you gone mad?' Mulla replied only two kinds of gifts are valued in this world. First one would be getting back one's lost object and second to give away one's most beloved thing as a gift to someone else. That is why I have put this advertisement.' To hear Mulla talk like this everyone was speechless.

We must remember that bad things do happen. How I respond to them defines my character and the quality of my life. I can choose to sit in perpetual sadness, immobilised by the gravity of my loss, or I can choose to rise from the pain and treasure the most precious gift I have–life itself.

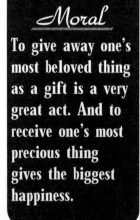

Moral
To give away one's most beloved thing as a gift is a very great act. And to receive one's most precious thing gives the biggest happiness.

a miraculous ring

King Chandrasen's popularity was quite far reaching in his kingdom and outside. In his kingdom there were highly knowledgeable scholars and learned men. One day king decided to judge their ability. He called all learned men and scholars in his court and said, 'I saw a ring in my dream. If I will wear that ring it will make me very happy, but if I will look towards it can make me sad as well. Can you people bring such a miraculous ring for me?'

But none of the scholars had the answer to the king's question. They found king's demand very un-usual. They thought where they could find such a ring. After a lot of discussion and reflection they decided to get such a ring made. After few days they gifted this ring to the king. King was very happy to wear such a beautiful ring on his finger. But as soon as he saw the ring carefully he grew sad. The learned men and scholars got this etched on the ring, 'one day this all will be destroyed.'

It is wise remembering that I will be dead soon is the most important tool I have ever encountered to help me make big choices in life. Because almost everything-all external expectations all pride, all fear of embarassment or failure-these things fall away in the face of death, learning only what is truly important.

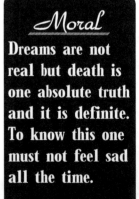

Moral
Dreams are not real but death is one absolute truth and it is definite. To know this one must not feel sad all the time.

betrayal is no one's friend

King Indrasen had a habit of listening to religious stories. This is why he appointed a story teller for his personal story sessions. He would come every day to narrate religious stories in front of the king. After listening to his stories king would give him a gold coin every day. One of king's court members did not like this act. He decided to make an evil plot.

One day finding a suitable opportunity he asked the story teller, 'what kind of a story teller are you? King drinks usually and you sit closer to him in order to tell him religious stories. This is how the air travels from his mouth to yours and it destroyed your religiosity. Now when you will come for your session tomorrow tie a piece of cloth on your mouth first then tell the story.'

Story teller felt that court member was right. As soon as he left the court member approached the king and said, 'Your Majesty! What kind of story teller you have appointed? He complained that you mouth sticks of intoxicants. From tomorrow onwards he will tie a cloth on his mouth and then he will tell stories.' To have heard this king grew angry. He decided to punish the story teller. Next day story teller came for his story telling session and after wards when it was time for the summary and learning to be told at the end of the story he said, 'betrayal is no one friend and the one who plots it has to suffer it as well.'

After listening to his story that day king did not give him one gold coin but rewarded him with two of them and gave him a letter and said, 'give this letter to my crime officer.' As soon as story teller was going outside he met the same court member. Story teller gave him one of his gold coins and said while giving, 'king has given a letter for his crime officer and I am somewhat in a hurry, so could you please drop it on my behalf?' the court member said 'yes why not.' He went straight to meet that crime officer with that letter. As soon as the officer read that letter which said 'as soon as the person who brings this letter his nose should be chopped off.' The officer held the court member and without any delay he chopped off his nose. This is how the court member received his due punishment for the crime of betrayal.

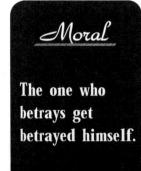

Moral

The one who betrays get betrayed himself.

30

VESSEL

*O*ne evening Mulla Nasruddin was cooking something in his kitchen. He felt a need for one new cooking vessel. But he did not have one so he went to ask for it from his neighbour. He asked for one vessel and promised to return it next day.

Next day when he went to his neighbour's house to return him his vessel his neighbour saw inside his vessel another smaller vessel of same kind was placed neatly. His neighbour asked, 'brother Mulla! Why another vessel is kept inside.' Mulla said 'last night your vessel gave birth to another smaller vessel, this is why I am returning both of them to you.' The neighbour got really happy with this knowledge and he accepted both the vessels from Mulla. After two or three days he went again to his neighbour's house to ask for a vessel. This time he asked for the bigger vessel. As usual his neighbour got happy with his request and returned his vessel back to him. He started to wait for the next day.

One week passed away but Mulla did not come to return the vessel. One day his neighbour and Mulla met each other in the market place. His neighbour asked him, 'where is my vessel?' Mulla replied, 'oh! That vessel has died.' The neighbour asked, 'how that can be possible? Can a vessel die?' Then Mulla said, 'why brother! If a vessel can give birth then it can die on its own as well.' After listening to Mulla's remark he understood his vessel is never going to return.

Moral

To act clever and to believe in impossible thing is the sign of utter foolishness.

broken pride

King Kulbhushan's daughter Vijaya was extremely beautiful but proud of herself as well. She could never talk to anyone politely and nicely. One day a saint arrived in the palace. He analysed lines etched on Vijaya's forehead and said, 'this girl's marriage will happen with the minister's son.' To hear this Vijaya got very angry. She immediately asked this saint to leave her palace. But king's minister had a son, his name was Anggad he used to like Vijaya a lot. One day he actually proposed Vijaya. But she insulted him and asked to leave the vicinity. He felt deeply hurt and humiliated and immediately left the city.

While walking he arrived at such a beautiful spot where every corner was green and soothing. He was appreciating that spot then all of a sudden he saw an elephant there, it was holding a garland in its trunk for him. And he has put that garland around Anggad's neck. Anggad could not understand what all was happening with him. To see him perplexed a man came up to him and said our king has died. And a saint arrived here who told us, in whosoever's neck kings' beloved elephant will put a garland will be our next king. Anggad accepted this new proposal and took the responsibility of the new king.

Two years passed. During some festivities Vijaya saw Anggad, and started loving him. She was not able to recognize him. To know his daughter's choice king Kulbhushan sent a marriage proposal of his daughter for the king Anggad. Anggad accepted this proposal and their marriage took place with a lot of pomp and show. When she went to Anggad's palace after their marriage Anggad said to her, 'I guess what saint has told you finally has come true. After all you got married to your minister's son.' To hear him talk like this Vijaya was astounded. When she looked carefully at him she recognised who he was. Then Anggad said again, 'you had thrown me and that saint out of your palace by insulting us. But whatever is supposed to happen by means of destiny no one can alter that ever.' To hear Anggad's remark's Vijaya wowed to change her behaviour, and she felt quite ashamed of her past acts.

Moral

To be self-absorbed in pride is not wise thing because you never know the person one has disrespected may turn out to be helpful in future

hurdle of a track

One upon a time, King Shorye ordered to place a huge stone right in the middle of the main road in his kingdom and he hid himself at a distance under a tree and started to wait whether some person will lift it to keep it off this road. From that road a lot of courtly members and traders have passed, but no one tried to lift it and some people went to the extreme and started to blame king's governance and bad roads in their country. Therefore no one tried to keep that stone off the track.

After sometimes, a farmer was passing from there. He was lugging huge sacks of grains on his back. He looked at that huge stone and thought, why it was blocking the road? Someone might as well get hurt if that person will fall on it. I must lift it from this road. He kept the sack of grains away and tried to lift that huge rock. After a lot of effort he was accomplished in moving it from the track.

When he lugged his sack back on this shoulder and turned around he saw, where there was stone now a bag of gold coins was lying at the same spot. He did not pick up that bag and started to walk away from it. Then he heard a voice, 'Dear brother stop now.' when the farmer turned around king himself was standing there. To see the king the farmer was scared thinking who knows what crime he has committed. King said, 'do not get scared, this stone I have placed on the track. I wanted to see how many people actually try to take of the hurdle which comes in their lives. But it is sad to learn a lot of people have passed from here but no one tried to lift this stone from here. And you have finally achieved this work. This stone was symbolic to the hurdles which come in any mortal life, this bag of gold is the symbol of the fruit of hard work and bravery which one gets after crossing that hurdle.' The farmer happily accepted that bag of gold coins and thanked the king while walking ahead on this road.

Any obstacle which comes in life needs to be taken care by hard work and determination, only then one gets a reward in form of wealth and it benefits other people as well.

Moral

One must know how to control himself and be determined to achieve his goal.

an outcome of undesired work

*I*n King Amratya Roa's kingdom a house contractor used to live whose name was Gyanchand. He has made several huge buildings. One day he said to the king, 'Your Majesty! Now I have grown old. And my strength to work further is getting low day by day. If you order me to leave then I would like to spend my remaining life in my village with my family.' King asked, 'what will you do in your village? Why don't you call your family here?'

Gyanchand said, 'Your Majesty! I also desire the same, but to keep them here I do not have a house of my own. I never got this much of time to get my own house made. Now I will go back and will get a small house made for myself.' King replied, 'if you desire to go, you may do that but before leaving make one last house for me.' Now Gyanchand couldn't alter king's desire at all. He said yes to the king but his heart was not fully invested in the construction of this house. He wanted to finish this work rapidly and wanted to return back home as soon as possible. He even did not care this time whether the work was going on well or not.

To learn the house was near completion, king showed his desire to check his new house. King said to Gyanchand, 'now you do not have to go back to your village. From now onwards your family will live in this house. I give you this house as a gift from me.' To hear all this Gyanchand was stunned. He thought all his life he has constructed such lavish homes, but later got vary from my own work. I should have made my house even more beautiful. I should not have showed such hurry to reap my own harvest. But now nothing could happen. He suppressed his desire.

It is truly said that never be in a hurry; do everything quickly and in a calm spirit. Do not loss your inner place for anything whatsoever even if your whale world seems upset.

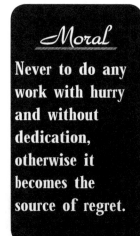

Moral

Never to do any work with hurry and without dedication, otherwise it becomes the source of regret.

search of god

*O*n the bank of a river a man named Dyanmagan was sitting. At the same time a young man came to him and greeted him with a lot of respect and said, 'I would like to be your student. Will you take me under your tutelage?' The teacher asked, 'why do you desire to be my student?' Then this young man replied, 'like you I also want to attain knowledge of God.' This teacher held his head and pushed it in the river. Young man tried to save himself for a while but he was helpless, after some time teacher left his head in the water itself.

The young man lifted his head out and started to breather heavily. After a lot of effort he become normal. Then the teacher asked him, 'when your head was in water that time what you wanted the most?' Young man replied, 'when my head was under the water that moment I was feeling suffocated and wanted to breathe air.' Teacher said, 'now return back home and come to me that day, when you will feel the need of God just as much as you have needed the air. On such a day I will take you under my tutelage without any examination or test.'

Knowledgeable people say that enlightenment is the key to intimacy and it is the key to itinerary. Everyone has a spirit that can be refined, a body that can be trained in same manner, a suitable path to follow. We must understand that we are here to realise our inner divinity and manifest our innate enlightenment.

Moral

To be that enlightened one must have such a profound desire to know God.

the real beauty

*K*ing Amaratyasen used to organise a prayer ritual for honouring God. For this ritual he would pick the most beautiful flower from his garden and would place it in the feet of the God. For this particular ritual a red rose was chosen in order to give homage over past few years. This is why the rose bush became very proud of it self. It started to feel that it is most beautiful thing in this world. Due to his pride he did not allow butterflies and honey bees to come near him at all. Right behind the rose bush a wild plant grew on its own. It had beautiful and bright yellow flowers.

It was a wild plant this is why gardener never paid much attention to it. This plant always allowed honey bees and butterflies to drink its nectar. All birds use to feel happy while sitting on its branches. Like all the years this year as well king came inside his garden to pick the most beautiful flower for this special ritual. To see him coming in the garden rose bush thought he would come straight to him and king cannot pick any other flower than him because 'I am the most beautiful flower of this garden.'.And the gardner escorted king towards the rose bush.

He said to the king, 'this year roses have bloom at their best they are even bigger than before.' To have said so as he approached the rose bush to pluck a flower, king stopped his hands and said, 'but this time I am looking for a different flower which is beautiful.' When he looked around he saw that wild plant which had yellow flowers on it. All butterflies and moths were hovering around it. On the other hand rose bush was standing alone. Kind went closer to that plant and said, 'gardner this is the plant which grew on its own without any care. You must have looked after all other plants. But this one has flourished on its own. You must have watered other plants and bushes on time and after a lot of effort they grow up to be so pretty. But this one stands here on its own courage. It is healthy and so beautiful as well. What is most important that butterflies are so happy to be around it. This is the mark of true beauty. Therefore for the ritual and prayers I chose this wild flower to be placed in the God's feet. King returned back to his palace after saying so and rose bush kept on standing there alone with a sullen face. But now its fake beauty and proud nature had vanished somewhere.

Moral

The one who survives on the power and their own might are the most beautiful creatures of this universe.

the neck of a camel

*O*ne day King Akbar felt very happy and pleased with Birbal's cleverness and presence of mind and declared to reward him. But a lot of days have passed and no sum of money was received by him. He was not able to figure out how to remind about this matter to His Majesty. So King Akbar went for a walk one day. And Beerbal was accompanying him too. Akbar saw a camel roaming around. To see its long neck twisted he asked Beerbal, 'tell me Beerbal why is it that a camels neck can be twisted in such a manner?'

Beerbal thought, 'there will be no better way of reminding His Majesty about the promise he made.' He said, 'Your Majesty! This camel must have promised a reward for someone and has forgotten about it for sure, this is why its neck is twisted. It is said that a person who forgets his promise then his neck gets twisted in this manner.'

To hear Beerbal's remark Akbar remembered his promise. He asked to Beerbal to come with him immediately and when they reached his palace he have him the due amount of money which he had promised as the reward. And asked, 'now my neck will not be twisted just as that camel?' Having said this he started to laugh. He knew by now Beerbal without asking for it has received his price out of cleverness.

The principal point of cleverness is to know how to value things just as they deserve. Appreciation of a person or a thing is the highest form of prayer, for it acknowledges the presence of good wherever you shine the light of your thankful thoughts.

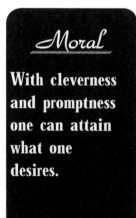

Moral

With cleverness and promptness one can attain what one desires.

the farmer and the king chandrasen

*O*nce King Chandrasen was returning home after winning a battle. He stayed right next to a village to rest. To see his soldiers distressed with hunger and thirst he commanded his army general to approach the nearing village. And said, 'go to the village and bring back the crop of biggest field possible.' The general with other soldiers went right ahead to find food. After walking some distance he saw a farmer there. He said, 'take us to the biggest field of this village.' And that farmer took them to a field. As soon as the soldiers started to chop of the harvest he said, 'you all must come with me to a different field. And you can take all its harvest.' And the general agreed with him. After walking a lot they saw a small field. The farmer escorted them to this field and said, 'if you wish you can have all its harvest.'

To see such a small field the general grew angry. He asked the farmer, 'are you a fool? We have left such a big farm to come down to this smaller one.' The farmer replied softly, 'I had no clue why you were asking for a field? The farm I took you first was not mine therefore I cannot decide for it. But this is my farm and I have full authority over it. To save my farm I cannot destroy someone else's field. This is why I have brought you here.' To hear farmer's talk general's anger subsided. He went back to see the king without bringing any crop and told him everything. To learn how farmer behaved the king was deeply impressed and rewarded farmer with a lot of gold coins and bought his entire harvest. Farmer was very happy to get money in lieu of his hard work.

Truly, what we do for ourselves dies with us. What we do for others and the world remains and is immortal.

Moral

The one who sacrifices himself is the greatest individual.

beauty and pride

Queen Rupmati was an amazingly beautiful woman. It was said when she drank water one could see it passing her delicate throat. Her beauty was known at all the places. She would often ask the king if there is someone prettier than her? To that king used to reply yes! You are the most pretty woman alive and most certainly my beloved and dearest one too'. So one day Rupmati said to the king, 'Your Majesty! Is there any one more beautiful than me?' but this time king did not reply. Rupmati kept on repeating the same question but king did not reply. He continued sitting quietly. The very next day Rupmati came in her fineries after getting dressed up specially for the king, 'Your Majesty, no one is prettier than me'. But the king did not reply again. She left that place immediately. Rupmati would ask the same question everyday but king will not answer her. After seeing king quiet for so long she got enraged and spoke, 'you would call me the most beautiful woman but now you avoid even replying to me.' Kind spoke after listening to her queen, 'did you ask me anything? You rather told me that no one is as beautiful as you. Earlier you would ask me this question whether any one is prettier than you or not? What you asked earlier it had a lot of fondness in it but now it shows your pride.' Rupmati learnt that day the fact it is beauty only that attracts everyone towards oneself, but to be proud of own beauty keeps other loved ones at a distance. Since then Rupmati never felt pride towards her beauty and the king started to praise her like before.

Moral

To go on repeating one self, people get silent after listening to it repeatedly.

the wealth of contentment

In a certain kingdom everyone was living happily. The king used to organize different kinds of tournament for his subjects, and he would honour every winner with a prize. This kept his subjects happy and excited as well. One day the king organised a competition to find a national champion. He got a new garden prepared. In this garden all sort of worldly things were kept. Every item placed here was of different value and cost. But no price or cost was written on them. The king announced that any person who comes out of this garden with the world's most valuable item will be declared the national champion.

A people went in to this garden and came out with a book, because for him knowledge was the most valuable thing. A poor man got out with a loaf of bread. For him bread was the most precious thing. One devout person came out with God's statue. For his God was the most precious thing. Amongst all these men there was a man who was very sagacious. He went to this garden but he did not come out with anything. The king asked him, 'what did you get there oh you the enlightened one?'

'I have got contentment with me your majesty', said the enlightened one. 'Is your contentment the most valuable thing present in the world?' asked the king. He replied, 'yes! Your Highness it is. Whatever you have kept there makes a mortal soul content. Any kind of contentment attained through objects are temporary therefore it is not complete or whole in itself.'

'That is half hearted contentment. The central point of this feeling of being content resides in the heart. And only such a person who has this central point in his heart, 'contentment' is the most valuable thing in the entire world.' King got very happy after listening to this man. Before declaring him a national champion the king called a meeting with his court members to understand what this man has said.

The meeting decided that contentment is the real meaning of life.

The king agreed with his court members to honour him as the national champion.

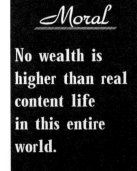

Moral

No wealth is higher than real content life in this entire world.

a blessing

*T*here was a place which had no inhabitant living. It had three mountains standing close to each other. There was a deep gorge around it. One day God decided to cross this place on his way to somewhere. To have seen God himself three mountains were adamant to get their wish granted as a blessing from the God. First mountain said please make me taller and the highest mountain at this place, so that if someone stands on me he should see all the places surrounding me to the further distance. Second mountain said that he desires to be full of riches and natural resources and beauty. So that people will get attracted towards me. And the third mountain asked there is a deep gorge right next to me please, make me so vast that I will breech this gap so that this space or gap can get filled and people could start coming and going from here again.

The God gave his blessing to the mountains. After a year to see the results of his blessings God came to this place again. He saw first mountain was so huge that people were unable to climb on it anymore. And the second mountain was inhabited by ferocious wild animals. It was full of natural beauty and resources now but people could not go there because of fear of animals. God saw the third mountain was no more at his original place. It had merged with that gorge. And the place where gorge was standing became plain. Now people started thronging that place and could inhabit it more often. Therefore God gave that place a name. For the gratitude's sake the third mountain scarified his own self so that it could benefit others hence his name was immortalised now.

Moral

For the life and benefit of others, a person who sacrifices themselves gains immortality forever.

destiney's aid

There was a town, a man lived who would sell things as a vendor in order to fill his children's stomachs. His name was 'Sujan'. Sujan would always use to say he lived by his hard work, hard earned money and by his destiny, but not by someone's charity. This matter reached king's ear and he decided to judge him. The king made Sujan his guard at the palace. He would watch the palace doors all day long but when evening approached he would get worried thinking about his children's evening meal. He found out a piece of wood lying nearby and he chiselled it kept it safely right next to his sword. He sold the piece of wood and fed his kids that day. King learnt about this incidence.

Next day king went on an inspection where Sujan was given duty to guard the gate. King started scolding one guard without any reason he said this guard's crime is unpardonable. He asked Sujan 'take out your sword and punish this man by chopping off his head from his body'. Sujan got panicked deep down but he used his cleverness and looked towards sky and said, 'if this man is innocent then turn my sword into a wooden sword.' The moment he took out his sword all the court people were amazed to see it was a miracle casted by God. King knew everything but he was also amazed to see Sujan's cleverness and he spoke, 'so it is indeed very true that we live by our hard work, cleverness and destiny, not by someone's charity.'

It is true that if you work hard then the result would be beneficial to you. Intelligent labour brings favourable results and ultimately leads to happiness.

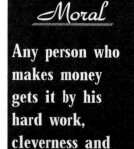

Moral

Any person who makes money gets it by his hard work, cleverness and what is given by destiny.

an innocent's punishment

*O*nce upon a time there was an academy where a king's son used to get his education. The prince was made to live like ordinary people and he was made to do all the work which any ordinary student to does. This prince would finish his entire task with full determination and would learn promptly whatever his teacher would make him learn. One such day the Prince has scored best in all his examinations. Now the time was to pay his education dues. With the prince other students were also required to give their due. From every one's home all their benefactors came in order to pay this due on behalf of the fellow students. The king also arrived with a band of people to attend the ceremony and give his son's education dues to the teacher.

In that ceremony the Prince was declared the best student of the academy. To have heard this King's chest swell with pride for his son. Prince went to receive his deserved prize. The entire place was echoing with claps and cheers for him. All of a sudden the teacher took his cane out and started beating Prince with it. Along with King everyone was amazed and horrified that in spite of giving Prince his reward, why the teacher was punishing him? Teacher immediately threw his cane away and embraced the Prince close to his heart and said; now his learning is complete. He said as a ruler he must know that someday he has to give verdict to a culprit but he must also remember how it is to experience pain and punishment when one is innocent and has not done a crime. Hearing this, the King had a very calming smile on his face.

Hearing thes, the king believed that the education is complete in all respects.

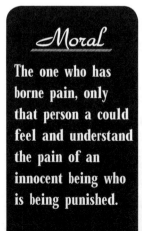

Moral

The one who has borne pain, only that person a could feel and understand the pain of an innocent being who is being punished.

the grand name but a small hearted presence

Long, long ago, there was a group of holy sages. Wherever they use to travel or settle around, they would survive on what they could gather through alms, therefore they always used to preach in the favour of people. They had heard about people of a city called Yashonagri and its great King Veerpratap's. He was known for his bravery. When they entered this city they were disappointed because there was no one who could give those sages alms, rather every one believed in taking favours here. Whichever house they went to, no one would open their doors for them, forget giving alms to them. They often pushed these sages away from their doorsteps.

These holy sages grew sad with all such practices and they were unhappy that people here have no kindness and faith in anything, not even a little bit of it which they can show to someone. They decided to approach their head called Premsukh in order to tell him about their troubles regarding this city. Premsukh said 'we must meet the actual head of this state which is the King itself.' First and foremost they were stopped by king's guards. After crossing all the hurdles willy-nilly, they reached to see the King. Before Premsukh could utter anything, King himself shouted at seeing them, and yelled 'how could a bunch of beggars have dared to enter my court?' By hearing him shout everyone started shivering with fear in his court. Then the holy sage Premsukh spoke, 'your highness I understood this before coming here, if there is no kindness and faith in the people of this city it is evident in the way this city has been governed.'

To doubt a beggar can be termed alright, which we understood long ago but not to be able to trust anyone even a little bit, comes to a mere fact that people here have lost faith in basic trust. Citizens do not show kindness towards any one here and where there is no kindness then there no faith can flourish either. By having said this all the sages started going their own way together out of this place. The name of such a popular city called Yashonagri is baseless and the popularity of its brave king is only futile, which holds no ground in reality.

Moral

A person who does not hold compassion of love, humanity, and faith, then all his great qualities are purposeless in this world.

river's water

King Shatrujeet's wife died. King was really sad and depressed. He left his kingship and started to say only one thing which is, 'someone please bring back my wife to me.' To see king in such miserable condition everyone got worried. King's grief spread in the entire kingdom and all his subjects started to mourn with him. Days and months passed by but the king was still suffering thoughts of his dead wife. Being continuously in grief king's health started deteriorating. First time in this kingdom such a sensitive issue had emerged.

After a lot of time king's old and trusted minister said to king that 'in his kingdom there is a village where a saint lived, he may be able to free you from your pain.' King immediately went there with his minister to see that saint. In that village the saint heard everything what king told him and said, 'I can bring your wife to you but for that you have to perform one task.' King replied 'to see my wife once more I can do anything.' Saint asked king to put one of his feet in the river and king did the same. The water of this river touched his feet and kept on flowing. The saint asked to repeat this procedure once more but kept one condition that he has to put his feet on the same spot in the same water as before. To that king spoke, 'I will keep my foot on the same spot but the water will not be the same as before. It must have gone ahead while flowing.' The saint said 'life's flow and speed is just the same. Place can be same but time has flown away which cannot be returned.' Shatrujeet understood this matter within the span of a moment and he came out of his grief and sad persuasion.

The king understood the fact of life that what's gone is gone for ever. It won't come back. If a toy made of mud gets broken, it can't be brought back no matter how much one tries.

Therefore there is no need to feel sorrow for what can't be undone. One must move with the flow of life.

Moral

Life's flow is ever changing; it cannot be stopped at one place alone.

Ugliness of Rupnagri

*T*here was very unique city called 'Rupnagri'. Rupnagri was called Rupnagri because here many beautiful women and handsome men lived. Everyone was endowed with immense beauty and handsomeness. Who so ever would look at them could not stop looking at all. As if God himself has opened a treasure box of beauty in this country. Having heard about the splendour of Rupnagri a man came there to see it. His name was Sawaliya. His complexion was dark. To see him there the entire city was completely surprised. All women hid their children away and men started to crack jokes about him and laughed at him. They pushed him and dragged him to their king's court.

King himself was very well endowed with handsomeness. When the king saw Sawaliya he could not manage to stop himself from laughing. And said, 'let him remain in this city, he will work on Rupnagri as a black spot sitting on a pretty face.' To this Sawaliya said 'it would have made me very happy king to live here as a black spot on this attractive city to save it from evil eyes but this city is smeared with black soot so how can anyone see a black spot on it?'

Now king's laughter turned into anger. He said, 'to claim Rupnagri as smeared or covered by soot why you would say such a thing?' Sawaliya said 'where people have vain glory for the blessing God had endowed on them, so much so that they have forgotten good manners due to their pride and vanity. People here are fair from outside but inside they are as black as soot, who will keep any relation with such people and place in future. Rupnagri's pride has destroyed its reputation.' Sawaliya's bitter remark opened king's mind. If internal bitterness is not being taken care then physical beauty on the surface does not matter or pleases anyone.

It is truly said that beauty is only skin deep. But unless the heart is clean and pure, facial beauty will never be appreciated.

Moral

If the physical appearance of face and body looks fair and bright enough but it is black and ugly from within then such a beauty is useless.

whatever happens, it happens for good

King Shamsher Bahadur enjoyed the sport of hunting a lot. During his entire hunting expedition the king's minister Gajraj Singh used to accompany him. He would help and guide the king during his hunting sport. Once while the king was shooting with his gun his horse got disturbed with the sound of shooting. The king fell on the ground and his little finger got chopped off during this accident. When Gajraj Singh saw it he went to the kings and said, 'Your Majesty, do not worry whatever happens, happens for good only.'

King did not like what Gajraj Singh said. First thing he did when king reached to his capital was he imprisoned Gajraj Singh immediately. Days went on passing and one day king had an urge to go for hunting again and this time he went alone. While hunting king looked for a prey and in its search he lost track and crossed into another territory. This was some native people's land. There were some rituals taking place in the native people's camp. They were about to offer a sacrifice. They were looking for a human being for this sacrificial right. They tied the lost king to a tree. The king felt very helpless. He could not do anything.

One of the native performing this right asked the head of the natives to chop off king's head and give it as on offering to the gods they believed in. As soon as the head of these natives lifted his sword to cut his head saw the king's missing finger. He told his fellow native that, 'we cannot offer this human being into sacrifice because one of his fingers is missing he is not suitable for this right. Let him go.' The natives let the king go away. Now the king had gained some strength and he had a sudden thought of his minister. First thing king did after reaching his capital was he asked Gajraj Singh to be taken out from his prison, he asked for his forgiveness and made him sit next to him, 'Gajraj Singh you were right! When you said whatever happens, happens for good only.'

It is said every action of God has some purpose. It we try to understand this purpose, we will always be happy.

Moral

It is true whatever god intends it happens for a good.

brainless imitation

*I*n the city of Ayodhya there lived a man called Churamani. To acquire wealth he prayed for long duration. After getting pleased by him the God of wealth and opulence, God Kuber himself came one night in his dream. He said 'at the time of sunrise stand at your doorstep with a tumbler full of water. A beggar will appear at your door. His one hand will have a bowl. As soon as you will touch that bowl with your stick it will transform into a gold one magically. You must keep it with you forever. To do such a thing for ten days you will have ten golden bowls at the end which will take care of your crisis and you will have a better life from now on.'

Every morning he would get up and start doing what Kuber had instructed him in his dream. One day a neighbour of his saw him doing so. Since that day his neighbour started to wait for the same beggar to arrive at his doorstep with a stick in his hand. After many days finally a beggar arrived at his doorstep, this man touched his golden bowl with his golden stick and it did not turn into the gold one. He repeatedly tried doing so but no success was seen. In the end he grew angry and without seeing here or there started beating this poor beggar. Within few seconds the poor beggar's life was lost in this ordeal. After knowing his crime this neighbour was punished for causing death.

Intelligence is something that cannot be copied. It is an innate gift given to us by God. We can use our brain to improve upon it. But it cannot be copied by any other person.

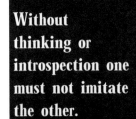

Moral

Without thinking or introspection one must not imitate the other.

the taste of sorrow

One of the king's court man was a very jovial and happy looking man. He would solve any problem with a simple smile of his. One day the king decided to ask him 'how is it that you always remain happy and smiling forever?' The court man replied by smiling 'Your majesty! I feed on sorrow.' The king did not understand anything but he said, 'if by tasting sorrow one become so jovial then I would like to feed on sorrow from now on.' To hear this the court man jerked his head gesturing 'no' and said, 'Your majesty! You will not be able to feed on sorrow it is rather difficult to savour it.'

King said 'what is it that I cannot do?' the court man said again with utter politeness that 'you will not be able to swallow it.' But king was hell bent on this matter and said, 'no matter how bitter is the taste of sorrow but if it can make a person happy throughout then I am willing to taste it.' The court man tried hard to explain to his king but he did not budge a little.

When king did not listen to him then his court man said, 'I have told you a small man cannot taste sorrow.' As soon as king heard himself being addressed as a small man king grew angry and drew his sword out in open and wanted to chop his head off. The court man said, 'see I told you that you cannot taste sorrow. On such a small matter you drew your sword.' To hear this king was ashamed and said 'you were right that small men cannot taste sorrow one needs a big heart to gulp down the taste of sorrow.'

Tolerance implies no lack of commitment to one's own beliefs. Rather if condemns the oppression or persecution of others. In fact, in practice of tolerance, one's adversary is the best teacher.

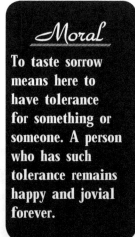

Moral

To taste sorrow means here to have tolerance for something or someone. A person who has such tolerance remains happy and jovial forever.

49

Mangoes

*O*nce upon a time a king had a vast orchard which bore a lot of mangoes on the trees. Those mangoes were really delicious and juicy. To taste them all court members were waiting for the right time. To feed those mangoes king decided to organise a big feast in which those mangoes were to be served. Before people could sit to feast on those mangoes an announcement was made that no one should be making any sound while sucking on to its pulp or its pit and neither a sound of licking one's fingers should be heard if someone will do so that person's head will be chopped off from his body. Everyone started to eat mango very quietly. Then suddenly king saw one of his court members sitting in one corner and was sucking on to the pulp of mango with all sounds and its juice was dripping from his fingers. King went to that man and said, 'did you not hear the announcement that no one will eat mangoes in this manner, otherwise that person's head will be chopped off?' That person answered with politeness, 'Sir! I have heard that announcement but such a succulent mango should be eaten by sucking out its pulp. Please let me have these mangoes just as I wish to have and once my hunger is satisfied you can get my head chopped off.' King grew very happy and said amongst all these men only one such being is present who knows how to enjoy life to the fullest. People who deprive themselves from all the pleasures of today waiting for another tomorrow to arrive do not live life to the fullest.

Learn to enjoy every moment of life. Be happy now. Don't want something outside of yourself to make you happy in future. Think how really precious is the time you have to spend, whether it's at work or with your family. Every minute should be enjoyed and savoured.

sword's man

In Japan lived a man his name was 'Matazuro'. His father was a very famous sword fighter. And he thought his son cannot be good sword fighter therefore he asked his son to leave his house. Matazuro became homeless and went to see a man named 'Bazo' who was also a famous sword fighter and asked him to teach him the art of sword fight. When Bazo saw him he asked him to work hard in order to learn sword fighting. To his remark Matazuro asked, 'if I will work hard then how much time will it take to become a skilled sword fighter?' the master said, 'your entire life.' Then Matazuro asked again, 'if I work harder than how much time will it take for me to learn it?' 'At least ten years', said Bazo. Then Matazuro replied, 'but my father is old and I have to take care of him in his old age. And if I devote more time than ever, how many years I have to spend learning it?' Bazo replied to his query, 'thirty years at least'. But how could this be possible? 'Earlier you said ten years but now you are saying it will take me thirty years at least. I have to become a great sword's man in lesser time.' Said Matazuro.

'I have told you thirty years because people like you who want results in a hurry do not get much out of learning.' To hear him say this, Matazuro said 'I will do as you please.' Bazo asked him, 'Get the idea of learning sword fight out of your head and learn to be a helper in my household.' From that day onwards Matazuro spent his entire day in taking care of Bazo's household. He would do everything in his house. He even left taking the name of swords and sword fight. He would get upset by seeing other students learning sword fight.

One day Matazuro was busy in his kitchen work, suddenly Bazo entered this kitchen quietly and attacked Matazuro with a wooden sword. But Matazuro stopped him then and there. From that day onwards Bazo decided to teach him sword fight. Within a short span of time Matazuro became a skilled sword fighter.

One day Matazuro asked Bazo, 'why did you refuse to teach sword fight earlier?' Bazo replied, 'in those days you had a desire to be great sword fighter within few days. Like several days feast cannot be eaten in one day, similarly a lot of days' hard work cannot be achieved in lesser time.'

Moral

With patience & hard work one can attain knowledge and only then learning is possible, but in hurry no one can learn anything.

STUDENT DEVELOPMENT/LEARNING

POPULAR SCIENCE

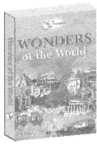

PUZZLES

DRAWING BOOKS

VALUE PACKS

COMPREHEANSIVE COMPUTER LEARNING (12410S)   SECURE A JOB (00600S)   QUIZ TIME (02312S)   (00223S)   (14001S)   (10305S)   (12211S)

All books available at **www.vspublishers.com**